MW00744105

A Lost Lamb
The Story of the Good Shepherd

We are grateful to the following team of authors for their contributions to *God Loves Me,* a Bible story program for young children. This Bible story, one of a series of fifty-two, was written by Patricia L. Nederveld, managing editor for CRC Publications. Suggestions for using this book were developed by Jesslyn DeBoer, a freelance author from Grand Rapids, Michigan. Yvonne Van Ee, an early childhood educator, served as project consultant and wrote *God Loves Me,* the program guide that accompanies this series of Bible story books.

Nederveld has served as a consultant to Title I early childhood programs in Colorado. She has extensive experience as a writer, teacher, and consultant for federally funded preschool, kindergarten, and early childhood programs in Colorado, Texas, Michigan, Florida, Missouri, and Washington, using the *High/Scope* Education Research Foundation curriculum. In addition to writing the *Bible Footprints* church curriculum for four- and five-year-olds, Nederveld edited the revised *Threes* curriculum and the first edition of preschool through second grade materials for the *LiFE* curriculum, all published by CRC Publications.

DeBoer has served as a church preschool leader and as coauthor of the preschool-kindergarten materials for the *LiFE* curriculum published by CRC Publications. She has also written K-6 science and health curriculum for Christian Schools International and gift books for the Zondervan Corporation, Grand Rapids, Michigan.

Van Ee is a professor and early childhood program advisor in the Education Department at Calvin College, Grand Rapids, Michigan. She has served as curriculum author and consultant for Christian Schools International and wrote the original *Story Hour* organization manual and curriculum materials for fours and fives.

Photo on page 5: Peter Cade/Tony Stone Images; photo on page 20: SuperStock.

© 1998 by CRC Publications, 2850 Kalamazoo Ave. SE, Grand Rapids, MI 49560. All rights reserved. With the exception of brief excerpts for review purposes, no part of this book may be reproduced in any manner whatsoever without written permission from the publisher. Printed in the United States of America on recycled paper. ✇ 1-800-333-8300

"God Loves Me" is a registered trademark of CRC Publications.

Library of Congress Cataloging-in-Publication Data

Nederveld, Patricia L., 1944-
    A lost lamb: the story of the Good Shepherd/Patricia L. Nederveld.
      p. cm. — (God loves me; bk. 39)
    Summary: A simple retelling of Jesus' parable comparing God to a
shepherd who loves every one of us and is happy when a wanderer
comes back to him. Includes follow-up activities.
     ISBN 1-56212-308-4
    1. Lost sheep (Parable)—Juvenile literature. [1. Lost sheep
(Parable). 2. Parables. 3. Bible stories—N.T.] I. Title.
II. Series: Nederveld, Patricia L., 1944- God loves me; bk. 39.
BT378.L6N43 1998
226.8'09505—dc21
                                         98-15641
                                            CIP
                                            AC

10 9 8 7 6 5 4 3 2 1

The Lost Sheep
The Story of the Good Shepherd

PATRICIA L. NEDERVELD

ILLUSTRATIONS BY PATRICK KELLEY

CRC Publications
Grand Rapids, Michigan

This is a story from God's book, the Bible.

It's for ^{say name(s) of your child(ren).}
It's for me too!

Luke 15:3-7

Do you know that Jesus loved to tell stories? People came from everywhere to listen.

One day Jesus told this story. . . .

There once was a shepherd, a kind and loving shepherd. His sheep knew he loved them because the shepherd took good care of each one.

Every day the good shepherd counted his sheep. He wanted to make sure they were all safe. For the shepherd knew that lambs sometimes wander away and get lost.

Sure enough! One day a little lamb did get lost. The worried shepherd looked for his precious lamb everywhere. Night came, and still he called through the trees for his lamb. He looked behind rocks . . . under bushes . . .

until he found it! Gently the good shepherd picked up the little lamb and carried it back home where it belonged.

"Good news! I found my little lost lamb!" the shepherd told his friends. Everyone was happy.

17

So was the lamb!

I wonder if you know that God loves you and takes good care of you every day and every night . . .

Dear God, thank you for loving us and taking care of us every day, every night! Amen.

Suggestions for Follow-up

Opening

Look for opportunities today to express your own love and care for your little ones. A smile, a word of appreciation, concern for their problems or hurts, a fair solution to a conflict—all of these will show them that in this place each child is cherished and safe.

As your little ones gather around you, ask if any of them have ever been lost. Or perhaps they've lost a special toy or precious blanket. Help them verbalize how scary and sad this can feel. Tell them that today's story is about a little lamb who is lost. As you read, pause at the end of page 13, and focus attention on the illustration of the shepherd. How does the shepherd feel? Wonder with them where the lamb could be and how the lamb might be feeling.

Learning Through Play

Learning through play is the best way! The following activity suggestions are meant to help you provide props and experiences that will invite the children to play their way into the Scripture story and its simple truth. Try to provide plenty of time for the children to choose their own activities and to play individually. Use group activities sparingly—little ones learn most comfortably with a minimum of structure.

1. Encourage children to reenact the story of the lost lamb at the sand table. (A large shallow box lined with a garbage bag works well for a sand table.) Using sturdy cardboard, cut out several sheep and a shepherd (see Pattern K, Patterns Section, *God Loves Me* program guide). Or use plastic or wooden sheep available at toy or craft stores. Provide twigs or craft sticks for bushes and pens. Talk about the shepherd's concern and care as children move the sheep around. Clap and jump for joy when the lost sheep is found!

2. Invite your little ones to dress up and play house. Look for opportunities to praise each one for taking good care of their family and pets. Ask the children if they know who is taking care of them both night and day. Help them say, "Thank you, dear God."

3. Play "Where Are the Sheep?" Ahead of time, make enough sheep (see Pattern K, Patterns Section, *God Loves Me* program guide) from posterboard so that each child will be able to find several. Ask the children to cover their eyes while you hide the sheep around the room. Then invite them to find as many sheep as they can find. (You may want to keep a few extra in your pocket to hide for a child who has difficulty finding some.) Help the children count the sheep they've found, and praise them for being such good shepherds.

4. You can use the sheep the children found to make a group mural. Copy and cut out the figure of the Good Shepherd (see Pattern Q, Patterns Section, *God Loves Me* program guide); color with markers or highlighters. Mount the figure on a large sheet of posterboard. If you wish, have children glue

stretched-out cotton balls to the sheep or just write each child's name on one sheep. Dab glue around the shepherd, and help your little ones place their sheep on the mural. Talk about how happy the sheep feel to be close to the shepherd who cares for them.

5. Play "Hide and Seek" with your little ones. This time ask the children to be the sheep while you are the shepherd. Close your eyes while your sheep hide themselves around the room. Count aloud slowly to ten. Then hunt for your lost sheep. As you find them, gently tap them on the shoulders and lead them back to the center of your room. When all the sheep are found, count them and give them a big group hug. Express joy that you have so many sheep to love.

Closing

Sing several stanzas of "God Is So Good" (Songs Section, *God Loves Me* program guide) as children follow your actions:

God is so good . . . (point up)
He cares for me . . . (point to self)
God loves me so . . . (cross hands over heart)
Thank you, dear God . . . (fold hands, sing prayer)
—Words: stanzas 1 and 2, traditional

At Home

Does your little one sometimes have trouble falling asleep? Sometimes even familiar bedtime routines won't calm a fearful child. Try reciting this reassuring prayer with your child:

Jesus, tender shepherd, hear me;
bless your little lamb tonight.
Through the darkness, please be near me.
Keep me safe till morning light.
—Adapted from lyrics by Mary L. Duncan, © 1963 by Singspiration/ASCAP. All rights reserved. Used by permission of Benson Music Group. Inc.

Old Testament Stories

Blue and Green and Purple Too! *The Story of God's Colorful World*

It's a Noisy Place! *The Story of the First Creatures*

Adam and Eve *The Story of the First Man and Woman*

Take Good Care of My World! *The Story of Adam and Eve in the Garden*

A Very Sad Day *The Story of Adam and Eve's Disobedience*

A Rainy, Rainy Day *The Story of Noah*

Count the Stars! *The Story of God's Promise to Abraham and Sarah*

A Girl Named Rebekah *The Story of God's Answer to Abraham*

Two Coats for Joseph *The Story of Young Joseph*

Plenty to Eat *The Story of Joseph and His Brothers*

Safe in a Basket *The Story of Baby Moses*

I'll Do It! *The Story of Moses and the Burning Bush*

Safe at Last! *The Story of Moses and the Red Sea*

What Is It? *The Story of Manna in the Desert*

A Tall Wall *The Story of Jericho*

A Baby for Hannah *The Story of an Answered Prayer*

Samuel! Samuel! *The Story of God's Call to Samuel*

Lions and Bears! *The Story of David the Shepherd Boy*

David and the Giant *The Story of David and Goliath*

A Little Jar of Oil *The Story of Elisha and the Widow*

One, Two, Three, Four, Five, Six, Seven! *The Story of Elisha and Naaman*

A Big Fish Story *The Story of Jonah*

Lions, Lions! *The Story of Daniel*

New Testament Stories

Jesus Is Born! *The Story of Christmas*

Good News! *The Story of the Shepherds*

An Amazing Star! *The Story of the Wise Men*

Waiting, Waiting, Waiting! *The Story of Simeon and Anna*

Who Is This Child? *The Story of Jesus in the Temple*

Follow Me! *The Story of Jesus and His Twelve Helpers*

The Greatest Gift *The Story of Jesus and the Woman at the Well*

A Father's Wish *The Story of Jesus and a Little Boy*

Just Believe! *The Story of Jesus and a Little Girl*

Get Up and Walk! *The Story of Jesus and a Man Who Couldn't Walk*

A Little Lunch *The Story of Jesus and a Hungry Crowd*

A Scary Storm *The Story of Jesus and a Stormy Sea*

Thank You, Jesus! *The Story of Jesus and One Thankful Man*

A Wonderful Sight! *The Story of Jesus and a Man Who Couldn't See*

A Better Thing to Do *The Story of Jesus and Mary and Martha*

A Lost Lamb *The Story of the Good Shepherd*

Come to Me! *The Story of Jesus and the Children*

Have a Great Day! *The Story of Jesus and Zacchaeus*

I Love You, Jesus! *The Story of Mary's Gift to Jesus*

Hosanna! *The Story of Palm Sunday*

The Best Day Ever! *The Story of Easter*

Goodbye—for Now *The Story of Jesus' Return to Heaven*

A Prayer for Peter *The Story of Peter in Prison*

Sad Day, Happy Day! *The Story of Peter and Dorcas*

A New Friend *The Story of Paul's Conversion*

Over the Wall *The Story of Paul's Escape in a Basket*

A Song in the Night *The Story of Paul and Silas in Prison*

A Ride in the Night *The Story of Paul's Escape on Horseback*

The Shipwreck *The Story of Paul's Rescue at Sea*

Holiday Stories

Selected stories from the New Testament to help you celebrate the Christian year

Jesus Is Born! *The Story of Christmas*

Good News! *The Story of the Shepherds*

An Amazing Star! *The Story of the Wise Men*

Hosanna! *The Story of Palm Sunday*

The Best Day Ever! *The Story of Easter*

Goodbye—for Now *The Story of Jesus' Return to Heaven*

These fifty-two books are the heart of *God Loves Me,* a Bible story program designed for young children. Individual books (or the entire set) and the accompanying program guide *God Loves Me* are available from CRC Publications (1-800-333-8300).